I am a Lemur

Aaron Carr

LET'S READ
AV²
BY WEIGL™
ADDED VALUE • AUDIO VISUAL

Go to www.av2books.com, and enter this book's unique code.

BOOK CODE

W585477

AV² by Weigl brings you media enhanced books that support active learning.

AV² provides enriched content that supplements and complements this book. Weigl's AV² books strive to create inspired learning and engage young minds in a total learning experience.

Your AV² Media Enhanced books come alive with...

Audio
Listen to sections of the book read aloud.

Video
Watch informative video clips.

Embedded Weblinks
Gain additional information for research.

Try This!
Complete activities and hands-on experiments.

Key Words
Study vocabulary, and complete a matching word activity.

Quizzes
Test your knowledge.

Slide Show
View images and captions, and prepare a presentation.

... and much, much more!

Published by AV² by Weigl
350 5th Avenue, 59th Floor   New York, NY   10118
Websites: www.av2books.com   www.weigl.com

Library of Congress Cataloging-in-Publication Data

Carr, Aaron.
 Lemur / Aaron Carr.
    pages cm. -- (I am)
 ISBN 978-1-4896-2633-2 (hardcover : alk. paper) -- ISBN 978-1-4896-2634-9 (softcover : alk. paper) -- ISBN 978-1-4896-2635-6 (single-user ebk.) --
ISBN 978-1-4896-2636-3 (multi-user ebk.)
1. Lemurs--Juvenile literature. I. Title.
 QL737.P95C37 2014
 599.8'3--dc23
                           2014038597

Printed in the United States of America in North Mankato, Minnesota
1 2 3 4 5 6 7 8 9 0 18 17 16 15 14

112014
WEP311214

Senior Editor: Heather Kissock   Art Director: Terry Paulhus

Weigl acknowledges Getty Images and iStockphoto as the primary image suppliers for this title.

I am a Lemur

In this book, I will teach you about

- myself
- my food
- my home
- my family

and much more!

I am a lemur.

I live high in the trees with my family and friends.

6

7

I like to have a ball
with my friends.

8

I bark and scream when
I have something to say.

10

I wave my smelly tail at other lemurs.

13

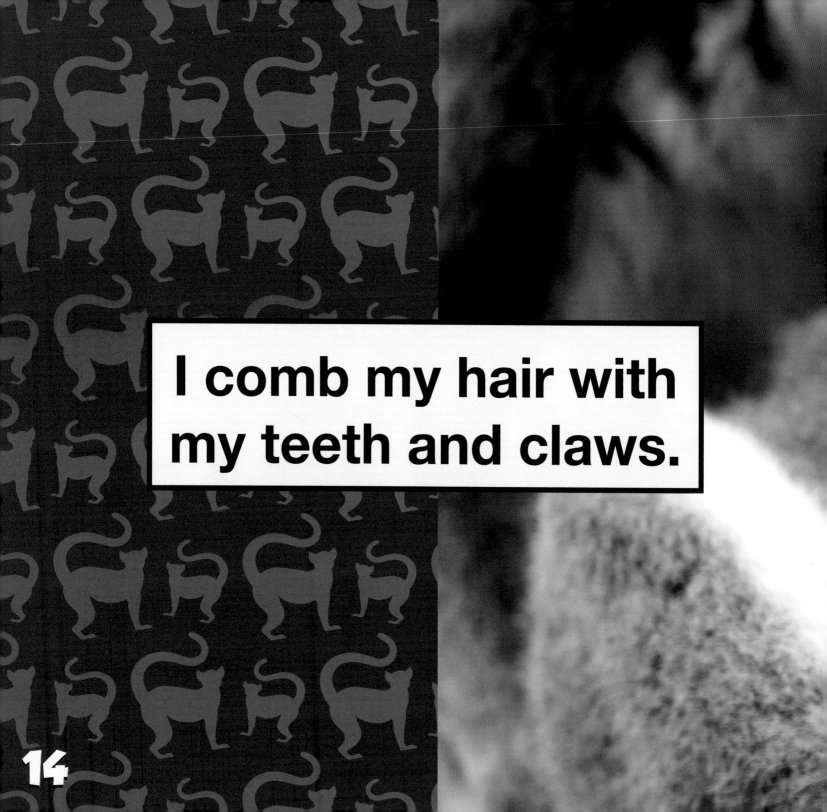

I comb my hair with my teeth and claws.

I stretch out in the Sun
when I need to rest.

I have eyes that glow in the dark.

19

I live in the forests of Africa.

I am a lemur.

LEMUR FACTS

These pages provide detailed information that expands on the interesting facts found in the book. They are intended to be used by adults as a learning support to help young readers round out their knowledge of each amazing animal featured in the *I Am* series.

Pages 4–5

I am a lemur. Lemurs are small- to medium-sized primates. There are about 100 species of lemurs. They look similar to monkeys, but have a long snout, which gives their faces a more foxlike appearance. Lemurs range in size from 3.5 inches (8.9 centimeters) long for the Madame Berthe's mouse lemur up to the 28-inch (71-cm) long indri.

Pages 6–7

I live high in the trees with my family and friends.
Lemurs usually live in groups, called troops. A troop may have up to 30 members, but between 13 and 18 is more common. Females are more dominant than males in troops. However, there can be different levels of dominance among both males and females within a troop.

Pages 8–9

I like to have a ball with my friends. Lemurs tend to be very social animals. They spend much of their time together, whether foraging for food, playing, or sleeping. Lemurs sometimes huddle together to sleep, forming what is called a lemur ball. This helps them bond while also keeping warm.

Pages 10–11

I bark and scream when I have something to say.
Lemurs can make 15 different sounds, each with its own meaning. A high-pitched scream often lets others know of danger. Mewing sounds may mean a member of the troop is lost. Lemurs also communicate visually by using facial expressions.

Pages 12–13

I wave my smelly tail at other lemurs. Lemurs also use scents to communicate. Male ring-tailed lemurs have scent glands on their upper arms. When males want to establish dominance over each other, they rub their tails on these glands. They then wave their tails at their opponents in what is called a stink fight. The lemur with the strongest smell is considered the dominant male.

Pages 14–15

I comb my hair with my teeth and claws. Lemurs groom each other regularly. Grooming keeps the lemur's fur clean and helps to strengthen bonds among troop members. The front teeth on their bottom jaw stick straight out to form a comb. A long claw on the second toe of each hind foot also acts as a grooming tool.

Pages 16–17

I stretch out in the Sun when I need to rest. Ring-tailed lemurs can often be seen sitting in the Sun with their arms and feet stretched out in a yoga-like pose. This helps to warm their abdomen, which has thinner fur than other areas. Sunbathing usually occurs in the morning, when the air is still cool.

Pages 18–19

I have eyes that glow in the dark. A lemur's eyes have a reflective layer inside called a tapetum lucidum. The tapetum lucidum reflects any light that enters the eye, causing a glowing effect and increasing the amount of light received by each eye. Lemurs do not have sharp eyesight, however, so they rely heavily on their strong sense of smell to find food and stay safe.

Pages 20–21

I live in the forests of Africa. Lemurs are one of the most critically endangered animals on Earth. They are found only in Madagascar and a few nearby islands. Humans are destroying lemur habitats in these places. More than 80 percent of the lemur's habitat in Madagascar has been cleared for lumber and agriculture.

KEY WORDS

Research has shown that as much as 65 percent of all written material published in English is made up of 300 words. These 300 words cannot be taught using pictures or learned by sounding them out. They must be recognized by sight. This book contains 25 common sight words to help young readers improve their reading fluency and comprehension. This book also teaches young readers several important content words, such as proper nouns. These words are paired with pictures to aid in learning and improve understanding.

Page	Sight Words First Appearance	Page	Content Words First Appearance
4	a, am, I	4	lemur
6	and, family, high, in, live, my, the, trees, with	6	friends
8	have, like, to	8	ball
10	say, something, when	12	tail
12	at, other	14	claws, hair, teeth
16	need, out	16	Sun
18	eyes, that	20	Africa, forests
20	of